Music Around the World

Patterns

Char Benjamin

Publishing Credits

Dona Herweck Rice, *Editor-in-Chief*; Lee Aucoin, *Creative Director*; Don Tran, *Print Production Manager*; Sara Johnson, *Senior Editor*; Jamey Acosta, *Assistant Editor*; Neri Garcia, *Interior Layout Designer*; Stephanie Reid, *Photo Editor*; Rachelle Cracchiolo, *M.A.Ed., Publisher*

Image Credits

cover Liveshot /Shutterstock; p.1 Liveshot /Shutterstock; p.4 Joel Shawn/Shutterstock; p.5 (top) Michael Rubin/Shutterstock, (bottom left) Jose Gil/Shutterstock, (bottom right) Sam DCruz/Shutterstock; p.6 GoodMood Photo/Shutterstock; p.7 Love Strandell/Shutterstock; p.8 Tom Grundy/Shutterstock; p.9 Marcel Jancovic/Shutterstock; p.10 M.E. Mulder/Shutterstock; p.11 Newscom; p.12 Peter Roan; p.13 Arturo Limon/Shutterstock; p.14 Mau Horng/Shutterstock; p.15 Bob Krist/Corbis; p.16 Peter Roan; p.17 Tohoku RM/Getty Images; p.18 Suzan Oschmann/Shutterstock; p.19 Robert Fried/Alamy; p.20 Jim Hughes/Shutterstock; p.21 (top) Jinlide/Dreamstime, (bottom) Drozdowski/Shutterstock; p.22 Marek Walica/iStockphoto; p.23 For The Post/Newscom; p.24 (top) IMSphotos/Newscom, (bottom) Leach/Shutterstock; p.25 Stephanie Reid; p.26 (top) Zentilia/Dreamstime, (bottom) Adele De Witte/Shutterstock; p.27 Stephanie Reid; p.28 Oliver Hamalainen/iStockphoto

Teacher Created Materials

5301 Oceanus Drive
Huntington Beach, CA 92649-1030
http://www.tcmpub.com

ISBN 978-1-4333-0421-7

Table of Contents

Music

People love to make music. Your feet will tap when you hear a march. Your hands will clap when you hear a drum.

There is a **pattern** to music. There is a pattern to the instruments that make music. It is the same all around the world.

West Africa

The body of a djembe (JEM-bay) drum is made from one piece of wood. The top is called the head. It is covered with goat skin.

Africa

The ropes around the drum are very important. They are used to tune the drum.

Djembe drummers play in patterns. The words *slap*, *tone*, and *bass* tell the drummer where to hit the drum. The *R* stands for right hand. The *L* stands for left hand. One drum pattern looks like this:

	R	L	R	L	R	L	R	L	R	L
bass	X	X					X	X		
tone			X	X						
slap					X	X				

a. What comes next—a slap, a tone, or a bass hit?

b. Which hand always starts the pattern?

Africa

The thumb piano has metal or bamboo keys. The long keys make low notes. The short keys make high notes.

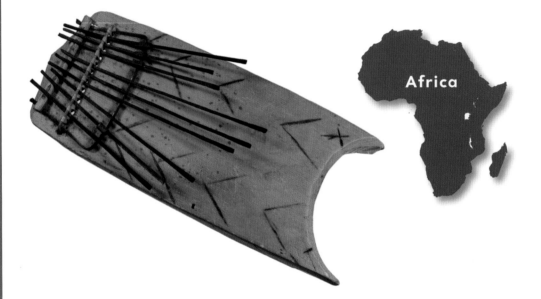

Africa

The thumb piano may be called different names. Here are a few:

Kalimba

Mhira

Sansa

It is easy to learn to play. You can make your own music in no time!

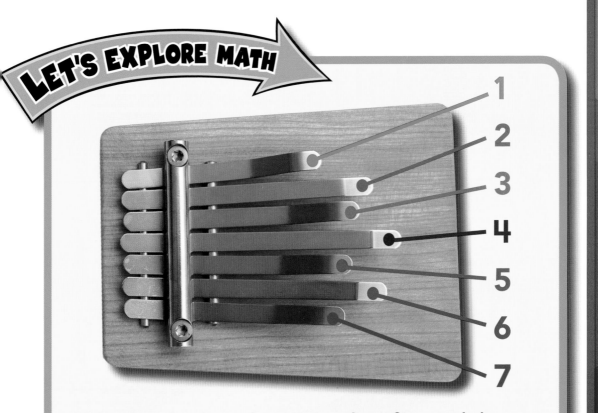

This thumb piano has a number for each key. They tell you which key to hit with your thumb. Here is a pattern for a tune:

4 4 5 4 4 6 4 4 5 4 4 ___

a. What key comes next?

b. What key is played for the 15th note?

Australia

A didgeridoo (DIJ-uh-ree-doo) is made from a hollow tree branch. First, termites eat the inside of a branch. The branch is cut off the tree. Then the bark is taken off. Next, a **mouthpiece** is made.

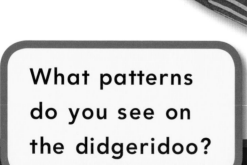

Australia

What patterns do you see on the didgeridoo?

Last, patterns are painted on it. A
long didgeridoo has a deep sound.
A short one has a high sound.

Iran

The daf is like a tambourine. It is round.
It is covered with fish skin or goat skin.
Metal rings are put inside the frame.

Iran

The rings in a daf
are called *zils*.

In the past, the daf was only played by women. Now men play it, too.

LET'S EXPLORE MATH

A tambourine is like a daf. Both instruments have zils. This tambourine has a double row of zils. The table shows the total number of zils in a tambourine with 2 rows.

number of sets	5	6	7	8	9
total number of zils	10	12			18

Copy and finish the table above. Then answer the questions below.

a. How many total zils are on a tambourine with 8 sets?

b. What pattern do you see in the number of zils?

China

The dízi (DEE-zuh) is a bamboo flute. It has 10 holes. There is 1 hole for blowing. The other holes are covered by fingers.

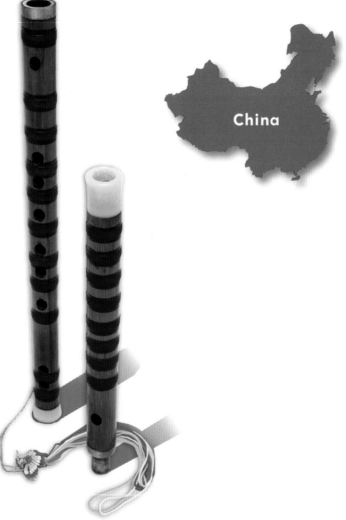

China

There is 1 hole covered by a thin bit of **reed**. This makes a buzzing sound when it is played.

Japan

The kotsuzumi (koat-sue-ZOOM-ee) is a small wooden hand drum. It is held on the shoulder. It is the shape of an hourglass.

Japan

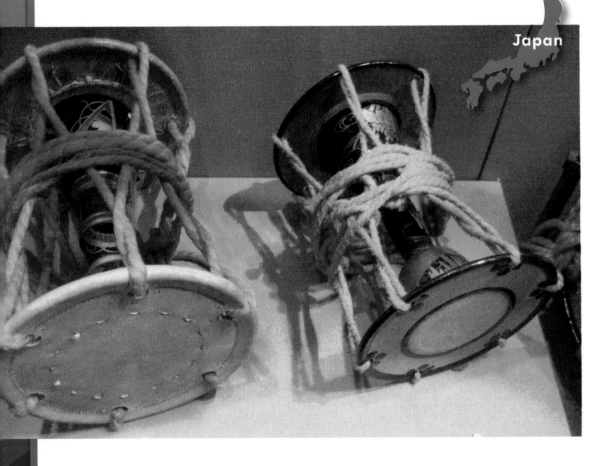

16

The 2 heads are covered with calf skin. Paint is used for the patterns.

Drummers often play in patterns of 4 beats. The table shows the pattern of a drumbeat. The big X stands for a loud drumbeat. The small x stands for a soft drumbeat. A pattern unit is the part of the pattern that repeats.

X x x x X x x x X x x ___

a. What is the pattern unit?

b. What type of beat comes next?

c. Draw your own beat pattern. What is the pattern unit?

17

Peru

The antara (un-tu-RAA) is a kind of flute played in Peru. Tubes of cane or bamboo are cut at different lengths to form this type of flute.

Peru

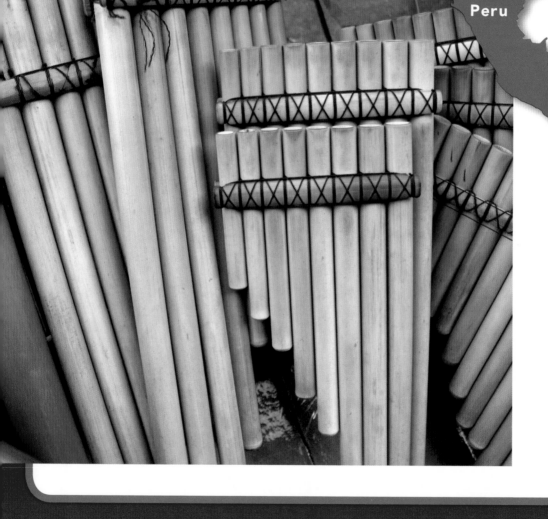

Long tubes make deep sounds. Short tubes make high sounds. The tubes are tied together in a curved or straight row.

Mexico

Maracas (muh-RAH-kuhs) are played in Mexico. These shakers are made from dried **gourds**. They have beans, seeds, or small stones inside.

Mexico

Whatever is inside affects how they sound when they are shaken. One of the maracas has a higher **pitch** than the other.

LET'S EXPLORE MATH

These maracas have a pattern painted on them. What color should be painted next to continue the pattern?

Italy

People made small flutes out of clay for thousands of years. They played just a few notes. The flute was called an ocarina (ok-uh-REE-nuh).

Italy

In the 1800s, a baker made a better ocarina. It had 8 holes in the front for the fingers. There were 2 holes for the thumbs in the back.

Ocarina means "little goose" in Italian.

Your Home

Do you want to make your own musical instrument? You can make a set of **claves**. All you need are 2 wooden dowels and some paint.

Paint a pattern on the wood. Tap them together to make a song.

You could even make your own drum. Get an empty coffee can and some paper.

Draw a pattern on the paper. Glue the paper around the can. Now make your own beat!

LET'S EXPLORE MATH

Look at this drum. It has a pattern around the outside.

a. What shape comes next?

b. What is the 12th shape in this pattern?

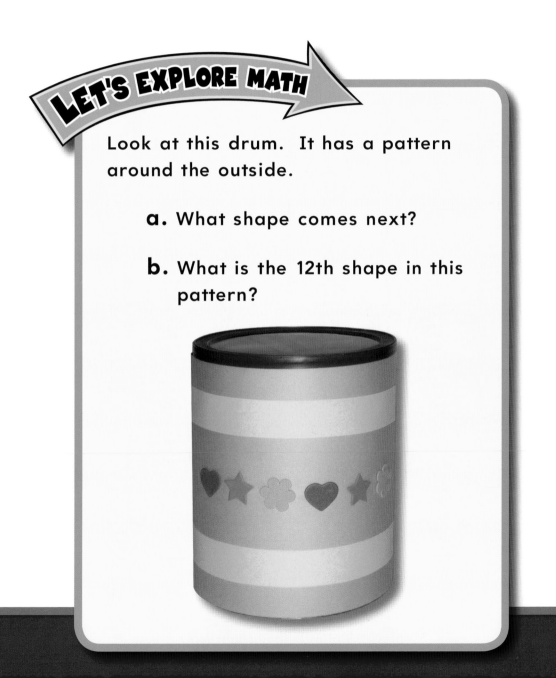

Decorating Maracas

Your music class is making maracas. Each maraca has a pattern around it for decoration. The music teacher wants you to make a pattern using 4 different shapes. What kind of pattern will you make? What is the 12th shape in your pattern?

Solve It!

Use the steps below to help you solve the problem.

Step 1: Choose 4 different shapes.

Step 2: Choose a pattern you would like to make.

Step 3: Use the shapes you chose to make your pattern.

Step 4: Repeat your pattern to find the 12th shape.

Glossary

claves—wooden sticks that are shaped like cylinders and are used as percussion instruments

gourds—fruit with hard rinds that grows on vines

mouthpiece—the part of a musical instrument held to the mouth

pattern—something that repeats itself many times

pitch—how high or low a sound is

reed—a tall, thin grass

Index

Let's Explore Math

Page 7:
a. tone
b. right

Page 9:
a. 6
b. 5

Page 13:
a. 16 zils
b. the number increases by 2 each time

Page 17:
a. X x x x
b. soft (x)
c. Answers will vary.

Page 21:
a. red

Page 27:
a. purple heart
b. orange flower

Solve the Problem

Answers will vary depending on the patterns created.